UNLOCKING YOUR PRODUCTIVITY POTENTIAL

Proven Strategies to Get More Done in Less Time

CASH GREY

Copyright © [2023], [Cash Grey]

All rights reserved. No part of this book may be reproduced, stored, or transmitted by any means without the written permission of the author.

This book is a work of nonfiction. The views expressed in this book are intended to provide helpful and informative material on the subject matter covered. The author has made every effort to provide accurate and up-to-date information. However, the author and publisher are not responsible for errors, omissions, or any outcomes related to the use of the material in this book.

TABLE OF CONTENTS

PAGE NO

COPYRIGHT……………………………………..ii

TABLE OF CONTENTS…………………………iii

INTRODUCTION ……………………………………..1

CHAPTER 1: Creating a Productive Environment …….. 4

CHAPTER 2: Develop a Morning Routine……………7

CHAPTER 3: Find a Workspace That Works for You … 12

CHAPTER 4: Time Management Strategies………….. 15

CHAPTER 5: Create a task List …………………….. 19

CHAPTER 6: Prioritize Your Tasks …………………….. 21

CHAPTER 7: Set Realistic Goals …………………….. 27

CHAPTER 8: Take Breaks 30

CHAPTER 9: Dealing with Distractions 32

CHAPTER 10: Eliminate as Many Distractions as ....34 Possible

CHAPTER 11: Schedule Time for Social Media 37

CHAPTER 12: Reconsider Multitasking 39

CHAPTER 13: Staying Motivated 42

CHAPTER 14: Celebrate Small Victories 44

CHAPTER 15: Reward Yourself 47

CHAPTER 16: Seek Support from Others 49

CONCLUSION 52

INTRODUCTION

Productivity is an important factor in life, whether it's in your job, home life, or personal pursuits. It is the ability to achieve the desired result efficiently and effectively. Being productive can help you reach your goals faster and reach higher levels of success. It can also help to create a sense of accomplishment and satisfaction in life.

If you are looking to become more productive and make the most of your time and energy, there are several strategies you can use. These include setting realistic goals, breaking up tasks into manageable chunks, creating a schedule and sticking to it, setting boundaries, and practicing self-care.

Setting realistic goals is the first step to becoming more productive. It is important to set manageable goals that you can achieve. This will help you stay motivated and focused on the task at hand. Breaking up tasks into manageable chunks is also key. This can help to make a big goal seem more achievable.

Creating a schedule is also important. Having a plan of action and sticking to it can help keep you on track and make sure you're using your time wisely. Setting boundaries is also important. This can include setting time limits for tasks, limiting distractions, and saying no to activities that don't further your goals. Finally, practicing self-care is essential. Taking breaks, getting enough sleep, and eating well can all help you stay productive.

These strategies can help you become more productive and reach your goals. With dedication and practice, you can start to see positive results and become even more productive in the future.

By following these strategies, you can become more productive and make the most of your time and energy. It takes a bit of practice, but with dedication and focus, you can start to see improvements in your productivity and reach your goals faster.

Good luck!

CHAPTER ONE

CREATING A PRODUCTIVE ENVIRONMENT

Creating a productive environment takes effort from both the individual and the organization, but it can lead to increased productivity and better results for both. A productive environment is one that encourages creativity, collaboration, and communication. It should provide resources and support that help individuals and teams work efficiently, while also providing a comfortable and motivating atmosphere.

The first step to creating a productive environment in an organization is to ensure that the physical space is conducive to productivity. This includes providing adequate space to work, ensuring that the workplace is well-lit and organized, and providing amenities like comfortable furniture and high-tech equipment. The physical workspace should be free of clutter and distractions and should be designed to maximize collaboration and communication between team members.

Next, it's important to develop policies and procedures that promote productivity. These should include rules for how work is to be completed, deadlines for completing tasks, and guidelines for how information should be shared and communicated. These policies should also provide clear expectations for employees and team members so that everyone is on the same page about what is expected of them.

In addition, organizations should create a culture of innovation and creativity. This can be done by encouraging employees to take risks, explore new ideas, and think outside of the box. Organizations should also provide resources and support for employees to help them become more productive.

This could include access to online training materials, development opportunities, and mentorship programs.

Finally, it's important to provide recognition and rewards for performance. This could include bonuses, awards, or other incentives for high-performing individuals and teams. It's also important to provide feedback and recognition for employees who are doing a good job. This can help motivate employees and foster a culture of productivity.

Creating a productive environment is an ongoing process that requires effort from both individuals and organizations. However, with the right approach, it can lead to increased productivity and better results for both.

CHAPTER TWO

DEVELOP A MORNING ROUTINE

A morning routine is a great way to set the tone for the day and ensure that everyone is on the same page and working towards the same goal. A morning routine can include tasks such as setting goals and objectives for the day, reviewing the day's tasks and deadlines, and reviewing the progress of any ongoing projects. It can also include activities such as meditating or exercising, which can help to reduce stress and boost morale.

By implementing a morning routine, organizations can ensure that their employees are motivated and organized and that they have a clear plan for the day. This will help to maximize efficiency and ensure that tasks are completed in a timely and productive manner. Additionally, a morning routine can help to foster collaboration and trust among employees, as it allows them to discuss their goals and objectives for the day and to come up with creative solutions to any potential problems.

Also, developing a morning routine is a great strategy for creating a productive environment in any organization. It helps to ensure that everyone is motivated and organized and that they have a clear plan for the day. Additionally, it helps to foster collaboration and trust among employees, while also providing them with the tools and resources they need to be successful; the following is the summarized list of a personal morning routine;

1. Wake up early: Start your morning by setting your alarm for a time that allows you to get up and start your day

with enough time to get ready and prepare for the day ahead.

2. Exercise: Take some time to get your heart rate up and exercise. This can be anything from a quick jog to some light stretching. Exercise can help to get your body and mind ready for the day ahead.

3. Healthy breakfast: Fuel your body with a healthy breakfast. This can be anything from a bowl of oatmeal with some fruit or a smoothie. Eating a healthy breakfast will give you the energy you need to start the day and stay productive throughout.

4. Get organized: Take some time to organize your day. Look at your to-do list for the day and plan out what needs to be done. Having a plan for the day will help you stay focused and on track.

5. Take some time for yourself: Make sure to take some time for yourself in the morning. This can be anything from reading a book, meditating, or journaling. Taking a few minutes for yourself will help to clear your mind and get you ready for the day ahead.

6. Get ready: Take some time to get ready for the day. Shower, get dressed, and get ready for the day ahead.

7. Connect with loved ones: Take some time to connect with loved ones. This can be anything from calling or texting a friend or family member or simply checking in with them. Connecting with loved ones can help to put you in a positive mindset for the day ahead.

8. Start your day: Once you've completed all of the above steps, it's time to start your day. Take some time to review your plan for the day and get to work.

By creating and following a morning routine, you will be creating a productive environment that will help you to maximize your productivity throughout the day.

CHAPTER THREE

FIND A WORKSPACE THAT WORKS FOR YOU

Finding a workspace that works for you is an important strategy for creating a productive environment. It involves finding a workspace that is tailored to the individual's needs, preferences, and lifestyle. This could mean looking for a workspace that provides an ergonomic chair, ample natural light, a quiet area for focus and concentration, or even a space that is close to home or work. It could also mean finding a workspace that has the right amenities, such as a coffee machine, a printer, or a comfortable lounge area.

This strategy is important because having a workspace that is tailored to the individual's needs and preferences can help to create a productive environment. When people feel comfortable and supported in their workspace, they are more likely to be productive and efficient. In addition, having a workspace that is tailored to an individual's needs can reduce stress and anxiety, which can also help to create a productive environment.

This strategy can also help to create a sense of ownership in the workspace, which can help to increase motivation and productivity. People are more likely to take pride in their workspace when it is tailored to their needs, preferences, and lifestyle.

Finally, this strategy can also help to create a sense of community in the workspace. When people have a workspace that is tailored to their needs, preferences, and lifestyle, they are more likely to feel connected to those around them. This can create a sense of camaraderie and collaboration, which can help to increase productivity and efficiency.

CHAPTER FOUR

TIME MANAGEMENT STRATEGIES

Time management strategies are techniques and practices that help an individual to manage their time effectively. These strategies are designed to help an individual to make the most of their available time, by focusing on tasks that have the highest priority, and delegating or eliminating those that are of lesser importance.

Time management strategies involve setting goals, planning tasks, and organizing schedules among others. Setting goals allows an individual to work towards their desired outcomes; planning tasks helps them to determine which tasks are most important to accomplish; and organizing their schedule allows them to better prioritize their tasks.

In order to effectively implement time management strategies, an individual must be able to identify and prioritize their tasks. This involves setting goals and objectives, creating a schedule and timeline, and defining the tasks that need to be completed. It also involves allocating an appropriate amount of time to each task and setting realistic deadlines for completion.

Time management strategies can also involve creating a task list, delegating tasks, or eliminating those that are of lesser importance. Delegating tasks can be done by assigning them to other individuals, or by outsourcing them to a third party. Eliminating tasks involves recognizing those that are of lesser importance and focusing more on the tasks that are of higher priority.

Time management strategies can also involve using productivity tools and techniques. These tools and techniques include using a calendar or to-do list, setting reminders, creating templates, and using time-tracking tools. These tools and techniques can help an individual to stay organized and focused and can help them to better manage their time.

In addition, time management strategies involve creating an environment that supports productivity. This involves eliminating distractions, setting boundaries, and creating a space that is conducive to productivity. It also involves setting a routine and sticking to it, and taking regular breaks in order to refresh and recharge.

Time management is a great way to stay organized, increase productivity, and reach goals. Implementing effective time management strategies can help an individual to manage their time effectively and make the most of their available time.

In addition, time management strategies are essential to effective time management. They involve setting goals, planning tasks, organizing a schedule, delegating and eliminating tasks, using productivity tools and techniques, and creating an environment that supports productivity. By implementing these strategies, an individual can make the most of their available time, and become more productive and successful. The proven techniques that are essential for time management will be discussed in detail in subsequent chapters.

CHAPTER FIVE

CREATE A TASK LIST

Task lists are an effective tool when it comes to time management. They provide you with structure, direction, and clarity in how you manage your time. In order to make a task list, you'll need to start by determining what you want to accomplish. This could range from completing a project or achieving a goal to simply making sure you get through your to-do list. Once you've identified what you want to accomplish, you can start by breaking the tasks down into smaller, more manageable chunks. This means looking at your task list item by item and breaking it down into smaller, more manageable steps.

Next, you'll need to assign deadlines for each task, which will help you stay on track and avoid procrastination. Finally, you'll need to track your progress. This can be done with a simple spreadsheet, or you may want to use a more advanced tool such as a project management system.

By following this process, you can create a task list that is both manageable and efficient. With a task list in hand, you can start to maximize your time and energy by focusing on the most important tasks first. This will help you achieve your goals faster and with greater efficiency.

CHAPTER SIX

PRIORITIZE YOUR TASK

Once your task list is broken down into its components, it's time to assign a priority to each item. Prioritizing tasks can be a challenge when there are many things to do and limited time to do them. It is important to be able to prioritize tasks in order to accomplish them in an efficient manner. Fortunately, there are a few different strategies that can help to make the process easier.

1. Time-Based Prioritization: This approach involves evaluating each task based on the amount of time it will take to complete. Tasks can be ranked in order of importance according to the amount of time needed to complete them. This strategy is particularly useful when there is a limited amount of time available or when tasks are closely related.

2. Urgency-Based Prioritization: This method involves ranking tasks in order of importance based on the urgency of the task. This strategy is useful when there are tasks that must be completed in a certain time frame. This could include tasks that are due on a certain date or those that need to be completed in order to meet a deadline.

3. Importance-Based Prioritization: This approach involves evaluating each task based on its importance to the overall goal or project. Tasks can be ranked according to how important they are in terms of helping to reach the desired outcome. This strategy can be useful when there are a variety of tasks that all need to be completed but not all are equally important.

4. Benefit-Based Prioritization: This approach involves evaluating each task based on the potential benefit it will

bring. This strategy can be useful when trying to decide which tasks to focus on first or which tasks to delegate to someone else. It can help to identify which tasks will bring the most benefit in the long run.

No matter which strategy is used, it is important to take the time to prioritize tasks to ensure that the most important tasks are completed first. By taking the time to properly prioritize tasks, it is possible to accomplish projects more efficiently and effectively.

Proven Techniques for Prioritizing Task

Prioritizing tasks is an important skill for anyone to learn, as it helps to ensure that tasks are accomplished on time. There are several techniques that can be used to prioritize tasks, depending on the individual's needs and preferences.

#1   Create a To-Do

One technique is to create a to-do list and rank tasks in order of importance. This can be done by assigning each task a numerical value or by simply writing down the tasks in order of importance. This helps to ensure that tasks are completed in the order that is most beneficial to the individual.

#2   the 80/20 Rule

A second technique is to use the 80/20 rule. The 80/20 rule, also known as the Pareto principle, is a concept that suggests that 80% of the outcomes come from 20% of the inputs. The 80/20 rule suggests that it is best to focus on the most important tasks and activities first. This means taking the time to identify the activities that will bring the most value, and then concentrating one's efforts on those activities.

By concentrating on the activities that will have the greatest impact, one can maximize their efficiency and get the most out of their time. This ensures that the most important tasks are completed first, and the less important tasks are left last. The 80/20 rule can be applied to nearly any situation and serves as a reminder to focus on the most important tasks and activities in order to achieve the desired results.

#3   Eisenhower Matrix

A third technique is to use the Eisenhower Matrix. This is a simple four-quadrant system that helps to prioritize tasks based on their urgency and importance. Tasks can then be organized into categories such as "Do First", "Schedule", "Delegate", and "Don't Do". This helps to ensure that tasks are completed in the most efficient way possible.

To create an Eisenhower Matrix, make a 2 x 2 square. On one axis, write "important" and "not important." On the other, "urgent" and "not urgent."

#4   the ABCDE Method

Finally, another technique is to use the ABCDE method. This involves assigning each task an "A", "B", "C", "D", or "E" rating. "A" tasks are the most important and should be completed first, while "E" tasks are the least important and can be done last.

CHAPTER SEVEN

SET REALISTIC GOALS

Setting realistic goals is a powerful time management strategy that can help individuals maximize their productivity and achieve their desired outcomes. Goals provide a sense of direction and purpose, enabling individuals to identify what they want to achieve and how they will do it. When setting goals, it is important to ensure that they are realistic and achievable; unrealistic goals can lead to feelings of frustration and disappointment if they are not met.

Realistic goals should be specific, measurable, achievable, relevant, and on time. An individual should be able to explain their goal in a few sentences and break it down into smaller, achievable steps. When setting a goal, it is important to consider the resources and support available, as well as any potential obstacles that may prevent the goal from being achieved.

Realistic goals should be challenging yet achievable. Individuals should take into consideration their current skill and knowledge level, as well as any time constraints that may exist. It is important to ensure that the goal is achievable within the given time frame and to not set the bar too high.

Realistic goals should also be relevant. Goals should be tailored to an individual's goals and values and should be meaningful and inspiring. Goals should be set with the intention of making progress towards something important, rather than simply trying to achieve a certain number or deadline.

Having realistic goals can help individuals focus their energy and efforts on the task at hand, and can motivate them to continue making progress toward their desired outcomes. Setting realistic goals can also help individuals develop better time management skills, as they learn to prioritize tasks and manage their time more effectively. By setting realistic goals, individuals can ensure that their time is spent productively and that their efforts are well-directed.

CHAPTER EIGHT

TAKE BREAKS

Taking breaks can be an important time management strategy. Breaks can help to restore focus and productivity, reduce stress, and improve overall well-being.

When it comes to time management, taking regular breaks can help keep you on task and prevent burnout. Breaks can give you the space to think about the task at hand and come up with creative solutions. It can also provide the opportunity to shift your focus away from your work and refresh your mind. Taking breaks can help you to maintain your focus and energy levels throughout the day.

When taking breaks it's important to ensure that they are productive and not just a form of procrastination. Try to focus on activities that will help you to recharge, such as going for a walk, listening to music, or doing a short meditation. If you need to take a nap or have a snack, make sure that you set a timer to ensure that you don't get too distracted.

Taking breaks can also be beneficial for your physical health. It can help you to reduce stress and improve your overall well-being. Taking regular breaks can help to reduce fatigue, reduce muscle tension, and improve posture.

Ultimately, taking breaks can be an important part of a successful time management strategy. Breaks can help to restore focus and productivity, reduce stress, and improve overall well-being. Make sure to take regular breaks throughout the day to ensure that you are able to stay on task and maintain your focus.

CHAPTER NINE

DEALING WITH DISTRACTIONS

Distractions can be the bane of productivity or the source of creative inspiration. Either way, it's important to learn how to manage them properly to stay on task and reach your goals. Dealing with distractions is a critical skill for anyone who wants to increase their productivity, whether in their personal or professional life.

Dealing with distractions is one of the biggest challenges that people face when trying to increase their productivity. Distractions can come in many forms, including emails, social media, phone calls, and even other people. It is important to understand how to manage distractions in order to maximize productivity.

The first step to managing distractions is to identify them. Take an inventory of the things that distract you from completing a task.

Once you have identified the sources of your distractions, you can begin to take steps to reduce them.

CHAPTER TEN

ELIMINATE AS MANY DISTRACTIONS AS POSSIBLE

Distractions can be a major roadblock to productivity and success. They can take away from the time and focus needed to complete tasks and reach goals. Therefore, it is essential to eliminate as many distractions as possible to better manage them.

The first step in eliminating distractions is to recognize what is causing them. Identify the activities, people, or environments that are leading to distraction. Once these sources are determined, it is important to create strategies to minimize the presence of those distractions.

Are you constantly being pulled away from your work by emails, phone calls, or social media?

Are other people in the office interrupting you?

Additionally, it can be beneficial to find activities that help to focus the mind and reduce stress, such as yoga or meditation.

Another way to reduce distractions is to create an ideal environment for work. This could involve setting up a dedicated workspace, free from clutter and other potential distractions. It can also be helpful to set specific goals and work in blocks of time. This will help to ensure that distraction-causing activities do not take away from productivity.

Finally, it is important to take breaks from work throughout the day. Breaks can help to reset the mind and help to maintain focus. Additionally, it can be beneficial to practice mindfulness and remain present at the moment. This will help to reduce the temptation to distract oneself with activities that are not necessary.

Overall, eliminating as many distractions as possible is an important tool in dealing with distractions. By recognizing the sources of distraction and creating strategies to minimize their presence, it is possible to better manage them and maximize productivity.

CHAPTER ELEVEN

SCHEDULE TIME FOR SOCIAL MEDIA

Scheduling time for social media as a means of dealing with distractions is a great way to ensure that you have time for yourself and for the tasks that need to be done. It is a great way to stay organized and keep yourself on track.

Firstly, Setting yourself a goal is crucial. How long do you intend to spend using social media? Do you want to limit yourself to a certain number of hours or minutes a day? Goals and limits ensure that you are staying productive and not getting too easily distracted. With some discipline and dedication, you can enjoy the benefits of social media while staying focused on the tasks that need to be done.

Once you have set a goal, decide how and when you will use social media. Do you want to check it once in the morning and once in the evening? Or do you want to check it throughout the day? Setting a schedule will help you stay organized and stop you from getting too easily distracted.

In addition to setting a schedule, it is also important to limit your use of social media. Try to focus on the most important tasks and set aside a specific amount of time for social media. This will help you stay productive and focused.

Finally, make sure to stick to your schedule. It is easy to get carried away when it comes to social media but if you do not stay disciplined, it can become a major distraction. Remember to stay focused and follow your plan.

CHAPTER TWELVE

RECONSIDER MULTITASKING

Just now, we discussed the importance of developing the habit of segmenting activities into manageable portions and setting manageable goals for each activity. We will now concentrate on each one separately. It's easy to slip into the multitasking trap when there are so many distractions around us.

Multitasking is difficult for people to do, according to studies. Stop attempting to accomplish 10 things at once! Your IQ decreases by an average of 10 points if you switch tasks more than ten times every day. You can complete activities more quickly and effectively by focusing on one thing at a time.

Multitasking is a popular way to try to deal with distractions. It is often assumed that multitasking is an effective way to handle multiple tasks or activities at once.

However, while multitasking can be a useful tool to help manage distractions, it is never an effective tool to deal with distractions; there are significant drawbacks to this approach.

First, multitasking can lead to a decrease in productivity. When a person multitasks, they are attempting to focus on more than one task at a time. This can result in important details being overlooked and tasks taking longer to complete. It can also lead to an increase in stress and fatigue, as multitasking can be mentally taxing.

Second, multitasking can lead to a decrease in the quality of work. When a person is multitasking, they are often not giving each task the attention it deserves. This can lead to mistakes and subpar work.

Finally, multitasking can also lead to a decrease in creativity. When a person is multitasking, they may be unable to think outside the box, as their attention is divided. A lack of creative thoughts and ideas may result from this.

In conclusion, multitasking is not an effective way to manage distractions, it has significant drawbacks. Therefore, considering the pros and cons of multitasking, it is important to decide it is not the right approach for dealing with distractions.

CHAPTER THIRTEEN

STAYING MOTIVATED

Staying motivated is a key component to increasing productivity. Being motivated helps to keep you focused, energized, and motivated to achieve your goals. Motivation is the drive that pushes you to take action and to continuously strive for success. Without motivation, it is easy to become complacent and lack creative ideas. It is essential to remain motivated if you want to be productive.

There are many ways to stay motivated, such as setting goals, celebrating small wins, rewarding yourself for accomplishments, seeking support from others, and having a positive attitude among others.

Staying motivated is a great way to increase productivity. It allows you to stay focused and energized and to achieve your goals. It is important to find what works for you and to keep motivated and on track. With the right motivation, you can unlock your potential and become more productive.

Setting goals help to provide direction and focus. Having a positive attitude is also important as it helps to keep you focused and motivated. Proven strategies for staying motivated are discussed in the course of this book

CHAPTER FOURTEEN

CELEBRATE SMALL VICTORIES

Celebrating small victories is an effective technique for staying motivated that is often overlooked. It involves taking the time to recognize and appreciate the little victories you experience in life, no matter how small they may seem. This could be anything from completing a task to achieving a personal goal. Celebrating your small wins acknowledges your hard work, helps you stay motivated, and encourages you to keep pushing forward.

The concept of celebrating small victories is especially valuable when it comes to dealing with failure and overcoming obstacles. When you experience a setback or failure, it can be easy to get discouraged and lose sight of your larger goal. By taking the time to celebrate the small wins, you can remind yourself of the progress you have made and your ability to accomplish things. This can help you stay motivated and push through the hard times.

Furthermore, celebrating small victories can have a positive effect on your mental and emotional well-being. Acknowledging your successes and taking the time to celebrate can give you a mental and emotional boost. This can help to increase your confidence and self-esteem, which can further help you to stay motivated.

In addition, celebrating small victories can help to build positive habits. When you recognize and reward yourself for the small wins, it reinforces positive behavior and encourages you to keep achieving. This can help to create a cycle of success and progress, which is essential to staying motivated in the long term.

Celebrating small victories is a great technique for staying motivated. Taking the time to recognize and appreciate the small successes in life can help to boost your mental and emotional well-being, reinforce positive behavior, and keep you motivated and pushing forward.

CHAPTER FIFTEEN

REWARD YOURSELF

Rewarding yourself as a technique for staying motivated is a great way to stay focused and productive. This technique involves setting short-term goals and then rewarding yourself when you reach those goals. By doing this, you can develop a sense of accomplishment and stay motivated to keep working towards your long-term goals.

The first step in this process is to set the goals that you want to achieve. These goals should be realistic and achievable, yet challenging enough to give you a sense of accomplishment when you reach them. You should also break down your goals into smaller, more achievable tasks that you can complete one at a time. You'll be able to stay motivated and focused by doing this.

Once you have set your goals, you can start to reward yourself. This could be anything from a small treat like a piece of chocolate or a cup of coffee to a bigger reward like a day out or a weekend away. It is important to find rewards that will give you the incentive to keep working towards your goals.

Furthermore, it is important to remember that rewards should be used to celebrate progress and motivate you to keep going. It is not a substitute for hard work but can help to make the process of achieving your goals more enjoyable and rewarding.

CHAPTER SIXTEEN

SEEK SUPPORT FROM OTHERS

Seeking support from others is a great way to stay motivated. When we have the support of those around us, we are more likely to stay committed to our goals and feel confident in our ability to achieve them. Having a network of people to turn to, for help and advice can give us the encouragement and strength to stay motivated.

One way to find support is to join a support group. Whether online or in-person, support groups can provide a great source of encouragement, motivation, and advice. They can help you stay focused, share strategies, and remind you that you're not alone in your journey. Additionally, they can be a great way to meet others who have similar goals and experiences, allowing you to build relationships and establish a strong support system.

You can also look to close friends and family for support. Having a friend or family member who can provide honest feedback and encouragement can make a huge difference in staying motivated. They can provide an outside perspective that can help you stay focused and on track.

Plus, having someone who knows you well and cares about your success can be incredibly motivating. When we have the support of people around us it helps us to stay committed to our goals and be confident in our ability to achieve them. It reminds us why we are pursuing our goals and helps to stay positive and focused.

Also, you can look for professional support. A coach or mentor can help provide invaluable guidance and advice.

They can help you create an action plan for achieving your goals and provide motivation to stay on track. Plus, they can help you identify any areas of weakness or obstacles that may be preventing you from staying motivated.

In addition, don't forget to seek support from yourself. Remind yourself why you're pursuing your goals, write down affirmations to stay positive and focused, and take time for yourself to recharge and recharge.

Overall, seeking support from others is an important part of staying motivated. Whether it's from a support group, friends and family, a coach or mentor, or even yourself, having a strong network of people who can provide encouragement and advice can help you stay focused and motivated.

CONCLUSION

There are many different ways to improve productivity ranging from creating a productive environment, managing your time more efficiently, dealing with distractions, and staying motivated. Each of these concepts requires a different approach and requires its own unique set of strategies as discussed extensively in this book.

Creating a productive environment requires the ability to set boundaries and eliminate distractions. This includes removing clutter, creating a comfortable environment, and finding ways to create a positive atmosphere.

Time management strategies are essential for optimizing productivity and making better use of our time. This includes setting daily goals and tasks, creating a schedule, and taking breaks.

Dealing with distractions can be challenging, as they can come from both external and internal sources. It is important to identify the source of the distraction and deal with it constructively.

Finally, staying motivated is essential to achieving productivity. This includes celebrating small successes, rewarding yourself, and seeking help from others.

By implementing the strategies discussed in this book, it is possible to create a productive environment, manage your time more efficiently, deal with distractions, and stay motivated. With dedication and commitment, it is possible to achieve success and live a more productive and fulfilling life.

Productivity is a skill everyone should strive to learn and perfect, anyone can benefit from it. By following these strategies and creating a positive environment, you can make the most of your time and reach your goals. You will have more time for the activities and people you love, and you will be able to achieve success in whatever you set your mind to. With the right strategies, you can unlock your potential and unlock a world of possibilities.

www.ingramcontent.com/pod-product-compliance
Lightning Source LLC
Chambersburg PA
CBHW050311220526
45465CB00005B/1943